Curriculum-Based Speech Therapy Activities

Volume I

All About Me

Todo acerca de mí

School

La escuela

Animals

Los animales

Family

La familia

Fall

El otoño

Friends

Los amigos

English and Spanish Edition

Bilinguistics, Inc.

Published by Bilinguistics, Inc.

For more information, contact Bilinguistics, Inc. or visit us at: www.bilinguistics.com.

ISBN-13: 978-1514860892

ISBN-10: 1514860899

INTRODUCTION

As a young speech pathologist, I was confronted with a caseload that was so large and staggeringly diverse that it nearly brought an immediate end to my early career. I worked across two campuses with 65 Spanish-speaking students and conducted evaluations on another five campuses. About a third of my students were in a half-day preschool program for children with disabilities. Many of my students had multiple disabilities.

I wasn't alone. The teachers I worked with had equally diverse classrooms and needed a better way to work with diverse students. The challenges of serving students from diverse backgrounds pose some of the greatest benefits and greatest difficulties of teaching. On one hand we are exposed to extremely unique and interesting cultures and the amount of impact you can make with each child is huge. On the other hand, we are never sure if a child is behind because he has not had exposure to a certain topic, is having difficulty working in a second language, or truly has a communication impairment.

I worked nights and weekends to keep up with paperwork and plan therapy and was rewarded that spring with an additional campus to cover a maternity leave. As bleak as this situation felt at the time, I now know that this a typical experience for educational professionals across the nation. These situations are challenging but they also provide us with a certain resolve and the perfect laboratory to create a solution. Speech-language pathologists and classroom teachers are able to work together to address academic goals and speech goals at the same time. The materials that lie ahead solve many of these issues by combining language enrichment strategies and academic concepts to effectively address communication disorders.

We can create materials that simultaneously enrich language skills and teach academic concepts. This way:

1) **We make no assumptions about a student's prior knowledge.**

2) **We give students multiple opportunities to practice their concepts in school and at home.**

3) **We don't waste precious time re-creating lesson plans and materials year after year.**

To solve the issue, I formed a working group with several speech pathologists to create language-rich materials and enlisted teachers from campuses across several districts to let us teach portions of the class and incorporate these language-rich materials into their classroom.

It is my hope that you find as much success with these materials as we have in supporting your teachers and moving your students through their goals.

Enjoy!

Scott Prath and the Team at Bilinguistics

HOW DO WE ENRICH LANGUAGE SKILLS THROUGHOUT THE DAY?

In order for this solution to be a success, we knew that it had to be something that could be synthesized into the current schedule of the day. That is why these language-rich lesson plans have been designed around 12 common academic activities.

Attendance / Greeting	Calendar	Song
Surprise Bag	Literacy	Articulation
Phonology	Mini Books	Table Activity
Crafts	Recipe	Game

WHY LANGUAGE ENRICHMENT IS IMPORTANT TO TEACHERS.

Children use their language to convey what they know. Teachers are responsible for presenting a topic and then measuring whether a child has learned it or not. However, if a child does not respond or is incorrect, how do we know if:

- the topic is unfamiliar to the student
- the student knows but cannot communicate his response effectively
- the student does not know

It all looks the same right? In each instance the student has either not answered or answered incorrectly. Language-rich activities provide support so students readily share what they know.

WHY ARE CURRICULUM-BASED THEMES IMPORTANT TO SPEECH PATHOLOGISTS?

The majority of students who receive speech therapy spend thirty minutes or one hour per week with their speech therapist. This equates to three percent of a child's academic day. That means that the majority of a child's time is spent with her parents and her teacher. We also know that the more ways (multi-modal) and times (opportunities) a child practices a skill, the more she will be successful.

By using classroom themes we not only access vocabulary topics, but we also provide a way for each student to practice newly acquired communication skills on a topic that she is familiar with. Plus, the homework provides greater communication opportunities through interactions with the parent.

INTERVENTION WITH YOUNG STUDENTS IS SUCCESSFUL WHEN IT:

- Aligns to the school curriculum
- Is multi-modal
  - Hands-on, table-time, floor time
- Has buy-in from all educational professionals
- Increases parent involvement

- Can be used in a variety of settings

  - Full-day, half-day, classroom inclusion, group therapy, individual therapy

- Takes into consideration second-language influence and low socio-economic status

TEACHER INVOLVEMENT IS CRITICAL.

- Children spend the majority of their time with teachers and parents and only a small fraction of their time with speech-language pathologists.

- The value that your student places on what you are teaching dramatically increases when the same words are used by their primary communicative partners.

- Frequency and consistency are two important principles that are achieved when parents, teachers, and SLPs focus on the same topic.

- Teacher buy-in and opportunities for them to work on your student's goals are greatly enhanced when you align therapy to the school curriculum.

PARENT INVOLVEMENT IS CRITICAL.

- Parents are the most consistent language models in their children's lives.

- Parents' use of language-based strategies leads to greater receptive vocabulary at 12 years of age (Beckwith & Cohen, 1989).

- Mothers' use of labeling and increased periods of interaction leads to increases in receptive vocabulary and greater expansion of expression in older children (Tomasello & Farrar, 1986).

- Participation by fathers in early childhood programs is beneficial to the child, father and other family members (Frey, Fewell, & Vadasy, 1989; Krauss, 1993).

- Empowerment leads to self-efficacy, or the belief that parents can make a difference in their child's development (Dempsey & Dunst, 2004).

- When families are involved in the intervention process, language enrichment is ongoing rather than during "therapy" only (Rosetti, 2006).

IMPROVE ACADEMIC SUCCESS AND REDUCE SERVICE TIME.

These lesson plans were developed by a group of bilingual speech-language pathologists who provide therapy services to young children and their families through home- and school-based programs. The goal of many young classrooms is to provide early intervention in order to reduce the need for future services and improve academic outcomes later on. In this model, it is not uncommon for the speech-language pathologist to see a student in individual or group settings using therapy materials chosen solely with the child's goals in mind. While this paradigm works well for a handful of students, we found that greater gains can be made when therapy aligns to the curriculum and when parents can interact with a child based on what they bring home from school.

WHAT'S INSIDE!

HOW TO BE SUCCESSFUL.

This is not just another book of lesson plans and speech therapy ideas. We know that our success was related to *what* we used in intervention but equally important was *how* we did it. We will share with you ways to be highly successful working with young children. We begin the book with the following sections:

- Getting Started

- Preparing for each lesson plan

- Pre-session setup—Getting Ready

- Session Overview— 30 minutes at a glance

- Visual Schedule Pictures

- Explanation of visuals/schedule and how to target goals for each

- Creating a schedule and choosing your targets

- Lesson Plan Templates

ACCOUNTING FOR DIFFERENT LEARNING STYLES.

We know that different students have different learning styles and when we teach across different modalities our students have greater success. We designed each unit to address a wide range of speech and language deficits, while incorporating songs, books, and floor- and table-activities.

The content of these units was driven by theory and research in the fields of child development, communication development, and early intervention. The lessons and activities in this book are based on Vygotsky's (1967) social learning theories. Social learning theories view social interaction as critical to development. Therefore, the entire professional team is seen as the child's guides, and the child is the apprentice who learns from the adult models (Rogoff, 1990). Strategies and activities in this book are based on Kindergarten curriculum, family involvement, and group interaction (peers) so that a child's primary social interactionists are key contributors to communicative behaviors.

GETTING STARTED

The visual schedule on the following page can be reproduced to schedule your day. Print and laminate the lesson plan components. Choose the activities for the day and use them to visually show progress and completion. Each theme includes a variety of activities to provide flexibility in intervention and all components can be completed in a single day.

LESSON PLAN COMPONENTS

The first two activities, attendance/greeting and calendar, are the same for every lesson. The other activities vary according to the theme. Activities may be chosen according to the needs of the students and desired length of the lesson. The first four activities are suggested to be done with all of the students in the class. For the following activities, it is optional to split the class into groups of three or four students to rotate through the other activities. This is ideal when the teacher and/or aide is able to participate in running the activities.

It takes one or several days to complete all of the activities in each section. This works great for the classroom setting. During small group instruction or during speech therapy, open each session with the calendar and/or greetings. Then choose one to three activities and close with a review. This way, fresh activities can be completed each session while remaining on the same topic to ensure repetition of vocabulary and concepts.

Do you have children with behavioral difficulties?

Professionals who work with children who have behavior difficulties know that poor behavior can be rapidly reduced if the child is "given" control of the situation. This visual schedule allows the child to choose his preferred activity *and* the order while working on activities the professional chooses. The child's choice is still on topic but he has a sense of control in making the decision.

Components

These activities can be completed in individual sessions or in small groups.

1. Attendance/Greeting	6. Articulation Station	11. Recipe
2. Calendar	7. Phonology Practice	12. Game
3. Song	8. Mini Books	13. Homework Sheet
4. Surprise Bag	9. Table Activities	
5. Literacy Center	10. Craft	

Visual Schedule Pictures

Cut out, laminate and put on a vertical Velcro strip.

Attendance/Greeting	Calendar	Song
Surprise Bag	Literacy	Articulation
Phonology	Mini Books	Table Activity
Crafts	Recipe	Game

Curriculum-Based Speech Therapy Activities

Attendance/Greeting *(10-20 min)*

The greeting activity is completed in the same way for every lesson. Select the activities and/or prompts based on your students' goals. This can be done with all students in the circle time area. Visuals for this activity are included on the following page. Show the name of each student to the group of students and have them identify the name. The chart below shows examples of how you can target goals during this activity.

Materials: Pictures and/or written names of each student. Attendance board

Adult	Students	Targeted Goal
Whose name is this?	David!	Who questions, literacy
Where is David?	Next to Anna.	Where questions
What sound does "David" start with?	/d/	Phonological awareness
Let's clap out the syllables.	Da—vid	Phonological awareness
Hi David, how are you?	Fine, thanks (shakes hand)	Greetings
Are you a girl or a boy?	Boy (sticks name under boy in attendance board)	Personal information
Put your name next to/under/over the boy.	(puts name on attendance board)	Following directions, spatial concepts
What would you like me to draw for your face? (draw face by name on attendance board).	I want eyes, nose...	Requesting, sentence expansion, labeling body parts, plurals

Calendar *(5-10 minutes)*

The calendar activity can be completed with all students at the start of every lesson. You can review the day, month, year, and current weather.

Materials: classroom calendar, weather visual

I am a boy.

I am a girl.

Curriculum-Based Speech Therapy Activities

Soy niño.

Soy niña.

CALENDAR

Cut out, laminate and use dry erase markers to mark the dates and month.

A weather visual is included on the right page. Cut out the weather square and arrow. Poke out the two holes and use a brad to fix the arrow to the center of the weather wheel.

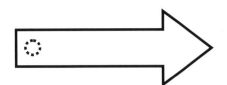

The Weather

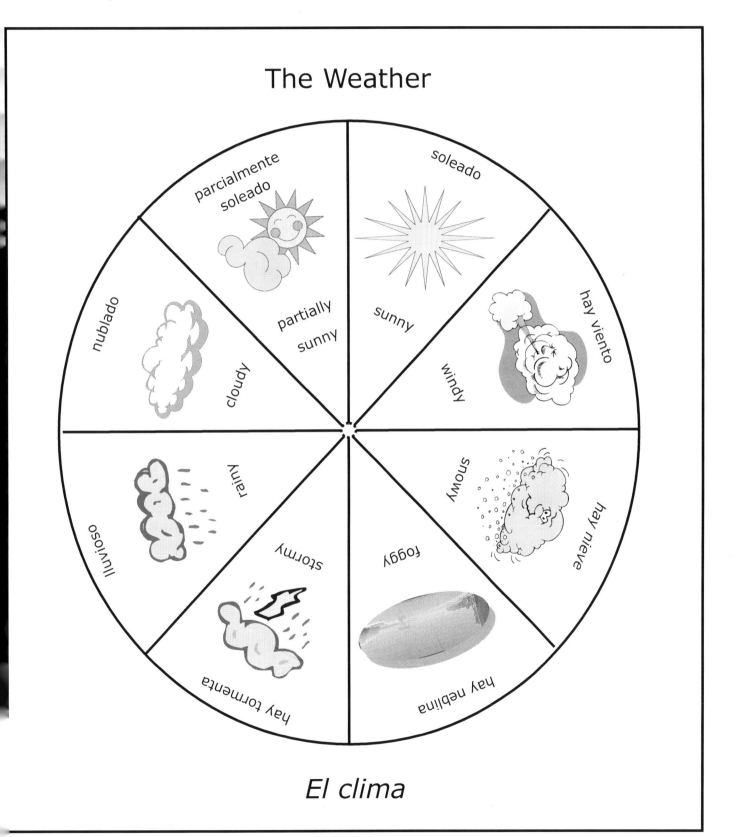

El clima

Song *(5 minutes)*

The song activity can be performed with one consistent song or songs that vary across the theme. If your group of students requires more repetition, sing the same song for every lesson. Songs about greetings, days of the week, or songs that have gestures are great choices. This activity is also a great break between seated activities. You can encourage participation by using hand signs and visual choices. If a student chooses more than one song, place the pictures on a board that says, "*first, then.*"

Examples of songs are found on the first page of each unit. To find more songs and visuals that go with the songs, visit http://bilinguistics.com/music-for-speech-therapy/.

Surprise Bag *(10-15 minutes)*

The purpose of the surprise bag is to introduce the theme and any relevant vocabulary. Allow the students to sit on the floor and take turns pulling a surprise out of the surprise bag. Surprise items vary according to theme. Each chapter includes picture cards (section A of each chapter) that can be printed and cut apart for quick lesson preparation. There are also suggestions for real objects to be used with each theme.

The following is a sample script with suggested goals:

SLP	Students	Targeted Goal
Close your eyes, put your hand in, and pull out a surprise.	(pulls out a surprise)	3-step directions
Whose turn is it?	*My turn*	Requesting, turn taking, *who* questions
What would you like?	*I want to get a surprise*	Requesting, sentence expansion
What do you have?	*A fish*	Labeling
What can a fish do?	*swim*	Object function
Please put the fish on the board.	(puts the fish on the board)	1-step directions

Literacy Center *(10-15 minutes)*

This activity can be done with all students or during small group rotation. The sample chapter includes book suggestions in English and Spanish that go along with the theme, as well as the Dewey Decimal System range for a quick library stop. Read the book to the students using scaffolding techniques. If applicable, increase interactions by using surprise bag items while reading.

Optional activity:

Gather both fiction and non-fiction books to provide a variety of pictures, references, and situations. Place a number of books related to the topic on the table. Encourage students to freely pick any book, look through it, comment, trade, and show friends what they see. Tell them they have two minutes. At the end, let the group choose one book that you look through (non-fiction) or read (fiction).

Articulation Station *(5-10 minutes)*

Review and practice targets from thematic articulation words in each chapter. You may prerecord the words so your students can listen to correct models and create an auditory station to use during small group rotation. Students may color the mini book or complete other table activity worksheets while listening. You can also listen to a recorded repetitions of the target word or allow students who have mastered the sound to demonstrate.

Phonology Station *(5-10 minutes)*

Have children identify the number of syllables in each word, and practice segmenting syllables by clapping or pointing to the circles under each word. Students may also work on identifying initial sounds. This can be done with the whole class or in small groups.

Mini Books *(10 min)*

While sitting at a table in a small group, students can make their own mini book about the theme. Students can work on sequencing the story, following directions to put the book together, and labeling pictures in the book. There are two examples of mini books included in each section.

Table Activities *(10 min)*

While sitting at a table in a small group, students can complete worksheets related to the theme. Teachers might also have worksheets that relate to the theme. Collaborate with the teacher to find out what kind of materials he/she has, and work with the students in small groups to complete the worksheets. Use language scaffolding as appropriate. Hone in on specific communication goals by working together and then target individual students' goals while the others are finishing minor tasks. Allow students who have mastered a task to demonstrate to friends how to follow instructions or complete a task. There are two examples of table activities included in each section.

Crafts *(15 min)*

Crafts are great for students who benefit from hands-on activities. Gather the materials listed at the beginning of each session and make the minimal preparations. Empower and challenge students by having them set up for the activity. Explain what they will be doing, show an example, and them ask for helpers to gather crayons, paper, glue, etc. Increase the level of difficulty by including numbers, an order, or descriptions of the materials. This activity is great for requesting materials, following directions, sequencing, and discussing what they did using past tense verbs.

Ask the initial helpers to gather and return the materials. Have each student stand, present his work, say something about it, and carry it to their backpack, folder, or cubbie.

Recipe *(20 min)*

This is another great idea for more active students who benefit from hands-on activities. Use sequence cards and visuals to help students request materials and describe what they are doing. Finally, have them tell how they created the end product.

Game *(5-10 min)*

Games are a great way for students to be exposed to theme-based vocabulary. A file folder game is included in each section. Another great game is to go 'fishing' by tying a magnet to a piece of string tied to a stick, and using it to pick up vocabulary cards that have a paperclip on them. You can also make multiple copies of vocabulary words and play a matching game.

Parent Note

Communication growth is stimulated by carryover into the classroom, vocabulary reviews, and shared participation by a student's teacher and parents. Write a note on a theme-based coloring sheet about what you are discussing in class, and what the parents can do to work on their child's communication goals at home. Reward a student for returning a signed parent letter to encourage communication and interaction with the family.

Note: To condense your lesson plan, you may choose either a mini book, table activity, craft, recipe or game to use for the lesson plan that day. You can then use the same lesson plan several times (or have the teacher implement it) using a different activity for each day.

PREPARATION FOR EACH LESSON PLAN

PRE-SESSION SETUP

Find out what topic of the week is.

Aligning intervention themes with classroom topics increases exposure and use of vocabulary. It also provides a framework in which students can practice their new language skills. Identify what is the current academic topic for the week (E.g., oceans).

2 minutes

Go to the library and check out books on the topic.

Using books to highlight a topic can empower students by giving them experience with the topic prior to practicing the skills that you are hoping for them to gain. Gather both fiction and non-fiction books to provide vast numbers of pictures, references, and situations.

10 minutes

Copy the activity pages for each student.

Communication growth is stimulated by carryover into the classroom, vocabulary reviews, and shared participation by a student's teacher and parents. Use these friendly activities and parent letters as your communication to strengthen your team approach.

8 minutes

Cut/color/copy materials needed for each session.

These sessions were designed for fast assembly and distribution. Gather the materials listed at the beginning of each session plan and make the minimal preparations. Better yet, have your students gather and prepare their own materials and bolster their receptive communication!

10 minutes

or

no time

PREPARATION FOR EACH LESSON PLAN

SESSION OVERVIEW - 30 MINUTES AT A GLANCE

EXPRESSIVE

Book Discovery (circle time activities)

Place a number of books on the topic around the table. Encourage students to freely pick any book, look through it, comment, trade, and show friends what they see. Tell them they have two minutes. At the end, let the students choose one book that you look through (non-fiction) or read (fiction).

7 minutes

RECEPTIVE

Pre-Activity Setup

Empower and challenge students by having them set up for the activity. Explain what they will be doing, show an example, and then ask for helpers to gather crayons, paper, glue, etc. Increase the level of difficulty by including numbers, an order, or descriptions of the materials.

8 minutes

EXPRESSIVE

Activity

Hone in on specific communication goals by working together and then targeting individual student's goals while the others are finishing minor tasks. Allow successful students to demonstrate to friends how to say a sound, follow instructions, or complete a task.

18–20

minutes

RECEPTIVE

Post-Activity Review (clean up, homework)

Ask the initial helpers to gather and return the materials they brought. Have each student stand, present his work and say something about it. They can then carry it to their backpack, folder, or cubbie. Reward a student for returning a signed parent letter to encourage communication and interaction with the family.

8 minutes

Lesson Plan Template (pg. 1 of 2)

Theme: _____   Date: _____

Below is an example of a lesson plan for a 2-hour class. Modify this lesson plan as needed to fit your individual needs, including time in the classroom and student goals.

Time	Schedule	Activity	Goals
20 min. 8:30-8:50	Circle Time Greeting/ Attendance 	Name recognition: Clinician holds up name card and kids find the student. Clap syllables of each name and focus on initial sounds. Clinician: **Whose name is on the card?** Students: **Jacob!** Clinician: **Where is Jacob?** Students: **Over there.** Clinician: **That's right. He is next to Keith.** **Okay, Jacob, where do I put your name? Under the boy or under the girl?** Clinician: **Okay, Jacob, what face parts do you want me to draw?** Jacob: **I want two eyes. I want a nose.**	Phoneme identification Syllables Who question Where questions Joint attention Spatial concepts Final /s/ Body parts SVO sentences
10 min. 8:50-9:00	Calendar 	Go over months in a year and then dance the Macarena while singing the months. Review days of the weeks, snap the days of the week song. Review the date. **Today is X. Yesterday was X. Tomorrow will be X.**	Sequences Numbers Categories Verb tense
5 min. 9:00-9:05	Language goal	**Today, we are going to learn about _____.**	1. Label: _____ 2. Verb: _____ 3. Target questions: _____
5 min. 9:05-9:10	Music 	Have the students choose between the following songs: Have the students dance the song, pairing gestures with key concepts.	Expanding utterances: "I want + to sing + ____"
15 min. 9:10-9:25	Surprise bag 	Place _____ in a bag. Have the students guess what kind of animals are in the bag. **Today we are talking about _____. What do you think is in the bag?** Pass the bag around and use the same sequence instruction for each student. **Close your eyes. Put your hand in the bag. Take out your surprise.**	Naming/labeling _____ Following directions

Curriculum-Based Speech Therapy Activities

Theme: _____   Date:_____

10 min. 9:25-9:35	Phonology	**Clinician: *We are also going to learn about saying sounds* _____.** Review picture cards with vocabulary from book that include phonology target _____.	1. Producing words that contain the sounds:_____ _____ 2. Clapping syllables of vocabulary words
15 min. 9:35-9:50	Literacy Center	Read the book _____ Expand on what a student is saying by adding words to what he says, offering him a good example and asking him to repeat, and asking him to complete your sentence: "Clifford is a *big* _____."	Label _____ Answer WH questions SVO sentence structures
30 min. 9:50-10:20	Centers: Each group spends 15 minutes at each station (Have teacher manage one station)	**Station 1: Articulation & Listening** Review articulation cards and discuss correct articulatory placement for bilabial sounds. (10 min). Target sounds in phrases to describe the vocabulary. Children will then listen to correct models of _____ while coloring _____.	1. Sounds: _____
		Station 2: Language Activity (Choose a mini book, table activity, craft, recipe or game. You may follow the same lesson plan but vary this activity each day).	1. Labeling 2. Requesting 2. Utterance expansion 3. Following directions
10 min. 10:20-10:30	Wrap it up and clean up	Review the language target and phonological target. Have students put the parent note in their backpacks. ***Today we learned about_____.*** ***We also talked about sounds we make _____.***	

All About Me
Todo acerca de mí

All About Me / *Todo acerca de mi*

SONGS

English	Spanish
Hello Friend	*Hola amigo*
Opposites	*Los opuestos*
Head, Shoulders, Knees, and Toes	*Cabeza, hombros, rodillas, pies*
Hokey Pokey	*Juanito cuando baila*
Ten Little Fingers	*Diez deditos*

Songs can be found at http://bilinguistics.com/music-for-speech-therapy/.

Book and Song Resources

BOOK LOCATOR

NON-FICTION

610 Medical Sciences

Title	Author
Froggy Gets Dressed / *Froggy se viste*	J. London
From Head to Toe / *De la cabeza a los pies*	E. Carle
Go Away, Big Green Monster! / *Fuera de aquí, horrible monstruo verde!*	Emberley
My Five Senses / *Mis cinco sentidos*	Aliki
Yo soy especial	S. Coan

All About Me Unit Content

Section	Schedule	Activity	Goals
A	Surprise Bag	Cut out body part picture cards Other options: • Mr. Potato Head • Stuffed animals • Animal puppets	• Following directions • Utterance expansion • What/Where questions • Turn taking
B	Articulation Station	Body part related words organized by sound for articulation targets Record target sounds for auditory bombardment	• Production of correct sounds in words and phrases
C	Phonology Syllable Strips	Body part picture cards in English and Spanish for 1-5 syllable words	• Syllable segmentation
D	Mini Book #1	I can do it! *¡Yo sí puedo!*	• Answer 'What doing' questions • Following directions • Sequencing • Utterance expansion
E	Mini Book #2	All about me! *¡Todo acerca de mí!*	• Following directions • Sequencing • Utterance expansion • Describing
F	Table Activity #1	Body parts functional relationships	• Describing functions • Labeling body parts and senses • Utterance expansion

All About Me Unit Content

Section	Schedule	Activity	Goals
G	Table Activity #2	Which Ones Are The Same?	• Following directions • Same/different • Labeling • 'Wh' and yes/no questions
H	Craft #1	The People Who Live in My Home	• Following directions • Labeling family members • Requesting materials
I	Craft #2	Pets in My Family	• Following directions • Basic concepts: part-whole, colors, numbers • Plurals (ear vs. ears) • Requesting materials
J	Recipe	Pretzel house	• Following directions • Requesting • Sequencing • Utterance expansion
K	Game	File Folder Game: Animal Homes	• Answering questions • Categorizing • Labeling • Utterance expansion
L	Parent Note	Family Coloring Page	• Demonstrate learning • Give parents visual cues to understand and converse with their child

Surprise Bag:
Body Part Picture Cards

A

ALL ABOUT ME

body	head	hair	eyes
cuerpo	*cabeza*	*cabello*	*ojos*
ear	nose	mouth	neck
oreja	*nariz*	*boca*	*cuello*
shoulder	arm	elbow	hand
hombro	*brazo*	*codo*	*mano*
finger	leg	knee	foot
dedo	*pierna*	*rodilla*	*pie*

Articulation Station

Use these words during any of the structured activities or in homework assignments to target a child's goals.

English

M   **m**outh, screa**m**, thu**mb**

P   **p**ants, ha**pp**y, hi**p**, jum**p**, li**p**

B   **b**ack, **b**od, **b**elly, **b**ack, eye**b**row, el**b**ow

K   **k**iss, **c**ough, **c**ry, **c**alm, **qu**iet, **s**cared, an**k**le, ne**ck**

G   **g**loves, **g**lad, an**g**ry

T   **t**ouch, **t**aste, **t**alk, **t**ooth, hur**t**

D   **d**rink, **d**ance, shoul**d**er, han**d**, hea**d**

F   **f**ace, **f**rown, **f**oot, **f**inger, **f**orehead, **f**ist, cal**f**, cou**gh**

S   **s**ee, **s**leep, **s**cream, **s**ad, **s**mell, **s**mile, no**s**e, wai**s**t, **s**cream

L   **l**egs, **l**ips, **l**augh, **l**ap, be**l**ly, e**l**bow, shou**l**der, eye**l**ash, ye**ll**, ank**l**e

R   **r**ight, w**r**ist, a**r**m, eyeb**r**ow, c**r**y, hu**r**t, hai**r**, ea**r**, shoulde**r**

Articulation Station

Use these words during any of the structured activities or in homework assignments to target a child's goals.

Spanish

M   **m**ano, **m**ejillas, **m**edicina, to**m**ar, co**m**er

P   **p**ie, **p**elo, **p**eine, **p**ierna, **p**estaña, **p**echo, cuer**p**o

B   **b**ostezar, **b**ailar, **b**rincar, **b**esar, **b**razo, **b**oca, **b**arbilla, **b**ufanda

K   **c**omer, **c**uerpo, **c**orrer, **c**antar, **c**uidar, **c**abello, **c**orazón, **c**omida, **c**ontento

G   **g**ustar, **g**uiñar, **g**ustoso, **g**arganta, **g**anador, **g**ordo

T   **t**os, **t**omar, **t**ocar, **t**oalla, **t**obillo, **t**riste, conten**t**o

D   **d**edo, **d**ormir, **d**ecir, **d**erecha, **d**ientes, cui**d**ar,

F   **f**laco, **f**alda, **f**rente, **f**eliz

S   **s**ed, **s**altar, **s**entar, **s**angre, **s**ueño, **s**oplar, **s**onreír, i**z**quierda,

L   **l**engua, **l**entes, **l**abios, **l**amer

R   **r**opa, **r**eír, **r**ubia, **r**izado, **r**odilla, sonreír

Phonology:
Syllable Strips in English

see
◯

eat
◯

sleep
◯

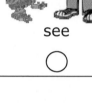

listen
◯ ◯

shoulder
◯ ◯

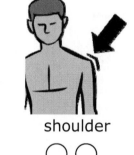

forehead
◯ ◯

different
◯ ◯ ◯

smiling
◯ ◯

crying
◯ ◯

embarrassed
◯ ◯ ◯

excited
◯ ◯ ◯

uncomfortable
◯ ◯ ◯ ◯ ◯

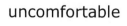

Phonology:

Syllable Strips in Spanish

ver

comer

dormir

llorar

gritar

frente

caminar

escuchar

◯ ◯ ◯

bostezar

◯ ◯ ◯

diferentes

◯ ◯ ◯ ◯

orgullosa

◯ ◯ ◯ ◯

emocionado

◯ ◯ ◯ ◯ ◯

Mini Book:

Color, cut, and create a book about yourself.

I can see with my eyes.

Yo puedo ver con mis ojos.

I can do it!

¡Yo sí puedo!

I can listen with my ears.

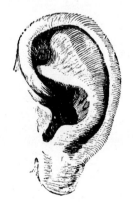

Yo puedo escuchar con mis oídos.

I can speak with my mouth.

Yo puedo hablar con mi boca.

Mini Book:

Color, cut, and create a book all about you.

I like to eat _____ .

All about me!

¡Todo acerca de mí!

Me gusta comer _____.

I like to play with _____ .

I am _____ years old.

Yo tengo _____ anos.

(draw candles)

Me gusta jugar con _____.

Table Activity:

Functional Relationships

How do you use these body parts? Match the pictures.

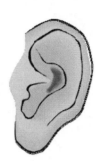

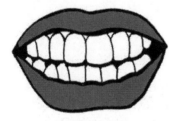

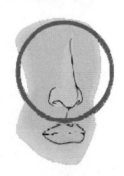

Curriculum-Based Speech Therapy Activities

Table Activity:

Let's Get Dressed!

Match the clothing item that goes with each body part.

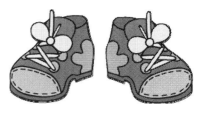

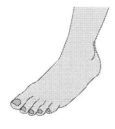

Craft:

Paper doll

Color, cut, and glue the clothes onto the paper doll.

Materials: crayons, scissors, glue

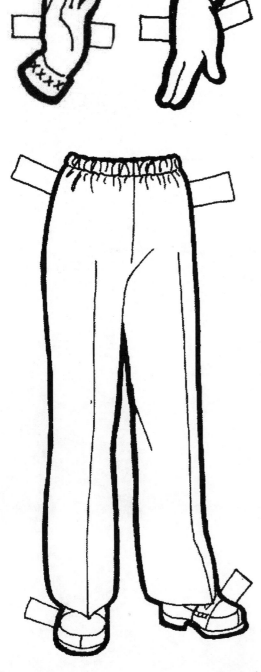

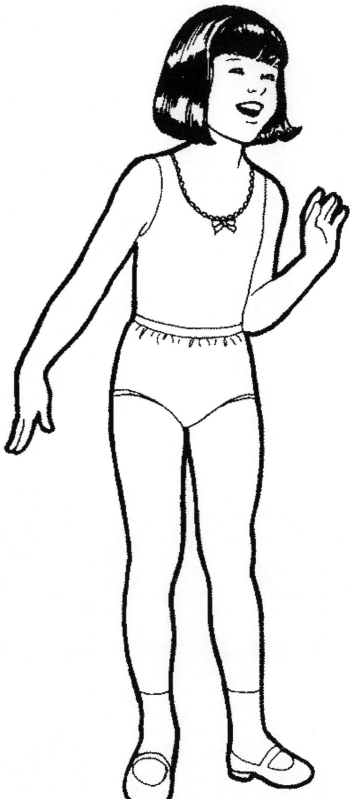

Craft:

Paper doll

Craft:
Monster Mask Making

Cut out shapes as body parts from colored construction paper, and glue onto paper plates. Describe each body part by color, size, and shape.

Materials: paper plates, construction paper, glue, markers

Curriculum-Based Speech Therapy Activities

Recipe:

Banana Man

In this activity you will use a banana as a body and insert 4 pretzels into the banana as arms and legs. Half a banana also works well for the body.   A wafer, cracker, or cookie can be inserted into the top of the banana as a head and extra banana pieces can be used as glue to glue on the raisin eyes.

Demonstrate how to make the banana man. Then use the activity to request, label, follow directions, and describe outcomes.

Materials: banana, pretzel sticks, vanilla wafers, box of raisins

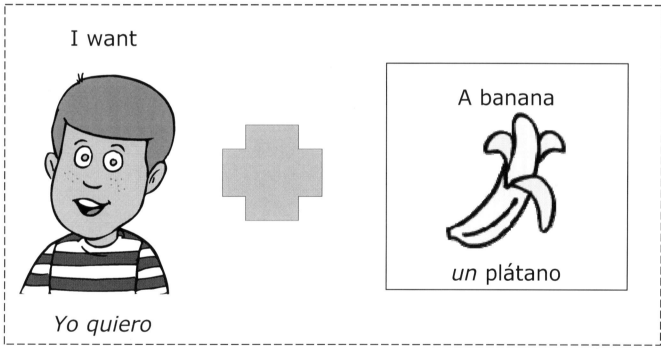

I want

Yo quiero

A banana

un plátano

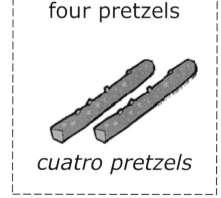

four pretzels

cuatro pretzels

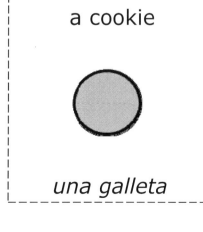

a cookie

una galleta

two raisins

dos pasas

Recipe:

Banana Man

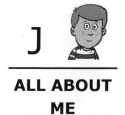
Demonstrate learning or pre-teach the activity with a sequencing activity.

Use the pretzels to make arms and legs.

Utilice los pretzels para hacer los brazos y las piernas.

Add two raisins for the eyes.

Utilice pasas para los ojos.

Peel the banana.

Pela el plátano.

Make the head with the cookie.

Utilice la galleta para la cabeza.

Game:

File Folder Game: Five Senses

Cut out and paste pictures on the inside of a file folder. Use Velcro or putty to stick pictures to their correct home (sights, sounds, smell).

Materials: two file folders, glue and Velcro or a plastic sandwich bag

Note: Pictures will cover both inside pages and a half page of the outside of the file folder. Use the extra room on the folder to mount the pictures on Velcro or tape a plastic sandwich bag to keep the pictures inside.

Game:

File Folder Game: Five Senses

I see/Yo veo

I touch/Yo toco

Game:

File Folder Game: Five Senses

**ALL ABOUT
ME**

I hear/Yo oigo

I smell/Yo huelo

Parent Note:

Picnic Coloring Page

Hi Parents!

This week we are talking about ourselves, our bodies, and how they work. Look at the picture with your child and talk about what we can see, hear, taste, smell, and touch.

¡Hola Padres!

Esta semana estamos hablando de nosotros mismos, nuestros cuerpos, y como funcionan. Miren a este dibujo con su hijo y pregúntale sobre lo que puede ver, oir, saber, oler, y tocar.

School

La escuela

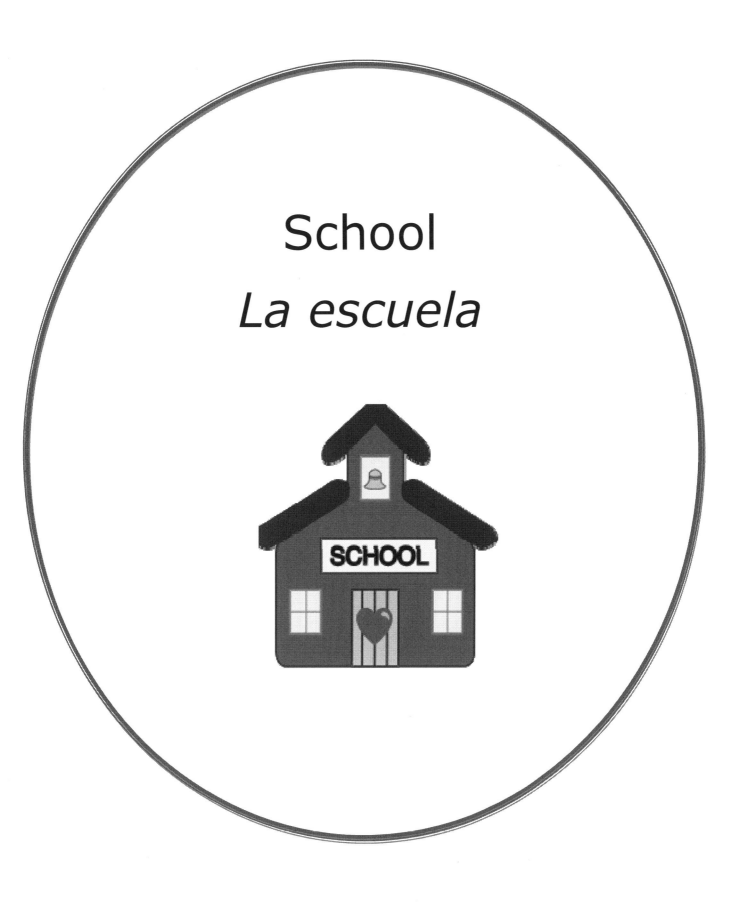

School / La escuela

SONGS

English	Spanish
It's Time for School!	*La escuela*
How Did You Get to School Today?	*Voy a la escuela*
I'm Crayon Crazy!	*Canción escuela segura*
I'm Ready for the First Day of School!	*Caillou - Canción libros*
Old McDonald	*La granja del Viejo McDonald*

Songs can be found at http://bilinguistics.com/music-for-speech-therapy/.

Book and Song Resources

BOOK LOCATOR

NON-FICTION

---

370 Education

Title	Author
Emily Elizabeth Goes to School *Emily Elizabeth va a la escuela*	Interactive Storybook teacher.scholastic.com
Franklin Goes to School *Franklin va a la escuela*	P. Bourgeois
El primer día de la escuela	B. Garcia Sabates
Froggie Goes to School *Froggie va a la escuela*	J. London
David Goes to School *Franklin va al colegio*	D. Shannon
If You Take a Mouse to School *Si llevas un ratón a la escuela*	L. Numeroff

School Unit Content

Section	Schedule	Activity	Goals
A	Surprise Bag	Cut out animal picture cards Other options: • School materials such as crayons, markers, tissue, paper, glue	• Following directions • Utterance expansion • Answering questions • Turn taking
B	Articulation Station	School-related words organized by sound for articulation targets Record sounds for examples of correct productions	• Production of correct sounds in words and phrases
C	Phonology Practice	School picture cards in English and Spanish for 1– to 5-syllable words	• Syllable segmentation
D	Mini Book #1	I Go to School *¡Voy a la escuela!*	• SVO sentences • First person verbs • Answering questions
E	Mini Book #2	Lunch Time *El almuerzo*	• Following Directions • Sequencing • Answering *what* questions
F	Table Activity #1	What goes together?	• Categories • Function of objects • Compare and contrast

School Unit Content

Section	Schedule	Activity	Goals
G	Table Activity #2	Who has more?	• Quantity concepts • Describing • Labeling
H	Craft #1	School Supplies Puzzle	· Following directions · Matching · Labeling · Requesting
I	Craft #2	What's in My Backpack?	• Following directions • Requesting materials • Size concepts
J	Recipe	School Bus Twinkie	• Following directions • Requesting • Sequencing • Utterance expansion
K	Game	Following Directions Dice	• Following directions • Directional concepts • Prepositional phrases • Utterance expansion
L	Parent Note	School Coloring Page	• Demonstrate learning • Give parents visual cues to understand and converse with their child

Surprise Bag:
School Picture Cards

classroom	playground	teacher	line
salón	*parque*	*maestra*	*fila*
paper	crayons	eraser	glue
papel	*crayones*	*borrador*	*pegamento*
scissors	book	pencil	tissue
tijeras	*libro*	*lápiz*	*pañuelo de papel*
rug	school bus	table	chair
alfombra	*autobús escolar*	*mesa*	*silla*

Articulation Station

Use these words during any of the structured activities or in homework assignments to target a child's goals.

B
SCHOOL

English

M   **m**usic, **m**ath, **m**arker, nu**m**ber, na**m**e, ga**m**e, costu**m**e

P   **p**aper, **p**aint, **p**encil, **p**lay, **p**retend, **p**uppets, **p**lay-doh, **p**layground, back**p**ack, hel**p**, ta**p**e

B   **b**us, **b**ackpack, **b**inder, **b**ell, **b**all, **b**lock, num**b**er, **b**oy, key**b**oard

K   **c**ut, **c**rayon, **c**olor, **c**ount, **c**lass, **c**omputer, **c**afeteria, ba**ck**pack, sna**ck**, boo**k**, blo**ck**

G   **g**lue, **g**irl , **g**ame, **g**rade, trian**g**le, ba**g**, ta**g**

T   **t**eacher, **t**race, **t**able, **t**ape, **t**riangle, cen**t**ers, le**tt**er, ar**t**, pain**t**, wri**t**e, ea**t**, coun**t**

D   **d**raw, **d**ance, fol**d**er, play-**d**oh, rea**d**, slide, bin**d**er, keyboar**d**

F   **f**lag, **f**irst, **f**riends, **f**older, **f**un, **f**ish, ca**f**eteria, lau**gh**, sa**f**ety

S   **c**enter**s**, **s**ci**ss**or**s**, **s**ing, **s**wing, **s**tory, **c**ircle time, bu**s**, re**c**e**ss**, dan**c**e, cla**ss**, tra**c**e

L   **l**ine, **l**unch, **l**isten, **l**etter, co**l**or, stap**l**er, tab**l**e, gir**l**, ha**ll** ba**ll**, be**ll**

R   **wr**ite, **r**ecess, **r**ead, **r**est, a**r**t, cafete**r**ia, pape**r**, colo**r**, teache**r**, lette**r**, numbe**r**

Articulation Station

Use these words during any of the structured activities or in homework assignments to target a child's goals.

B

SCHOOL

Spanish

M **m**úsica, **m**aestro, **m**esa, **m**ochila, nú**m**ero, no**m**bre, co**m**er, a**m**igos, pega**m**ento, ca**m**pana

P **p**egamento, **p**apel, **p**intura, **p**lastilina, **p**arque, **p**elota, cam**p**ana, **p**intar, **p**asillo

B **b**loque, **b**orrador, **b**año, **b**andera, **b**ur**b**ujas, li**b**ro, di**b**ujar

K **c**ampana, **c**omer, **c**olumpio, **c**ortar, **c**olor, **c**ontar, **c**uento, **c**lase, **c**afetería, es**c**uela, blo**qu**e

G **g**oma, **g**rapadora, ami**g**os, ju**g**ar, jue**g**o, pe**g**ar

T **t**ijeras, **t**iza, **t**eclado, **t**ítere, **t**razar, pin**t**ura, con**t**ar, cuen**t**o, le**t**ra, cin**t**a, pelo**t**a, carpe**t**a

D **d**ibujar, **d**isfraz, **d**escanso, ayu**d**a, marca**d**or, ban**d**era, tecla**d**o

F **f**ila, ca**f**etería, al**f**ombra, per**f**oradora, dis**f**raz

S **s**illa, **c**inta, **c**entro**s**, me**s**a, pa**s**illo, autobú**s**, pi**z**arrón, lápi**z**, tijera**s**

L **l**ápiz, **l**ibro, **l**etra, pape**l**, co**l**or, pe**l**ota, a**l**muerzo, tec**l**ado

R **r**ecreo, a**r**te, núme**r**o, títe**r**e, bande**r**a, juga**r**, pega**r**

Phonology:
Syllable Strips in English

paint

○

bell

○

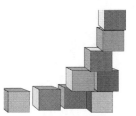

blocks

○

markers

○ ○

letters

○ ○

backpack

○ ○

library

○ ○ ○

principal

○ ○ ○

computer

○ ○ ○

librarian

○ ○ ○

cafeteria

○ ○ ○ ○

gymnasium

○ ○ ○ ○

Curriculum-Based Speech Therapy Activities

Phonology:
Syllable Strips in Spanish

letras
○ ○

puerta
○ ○

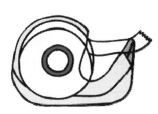

cinta
○ ○

mochila
○ ○ ○

campana
○ ○ ○

pintura
○ ○ ○

biblioteca
○ ○ ○ ○

marcadores
○ ○ ○ ○

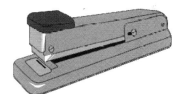

grapadora
○ ○ ○ ○

computadora
○ ○ ○ ○ ○

escritorio
○ ○ ○ ○

cafetería
○ ○ ○ ○

Mini Book:

Cut, color, and create a book about school.

I Go to School!

¡Voy a la escuela!

At school, I play with my friends.

En la escuela, juego con mis amigos.

At school, I sing songs.

En la escuela, canto canciones.

At school, I draw pictures.

En la escuela, yo dibujo.

Mini Book:

Cut, color, and create a book about school.

Lunch Time

El almuerzo

First I wash my hands.

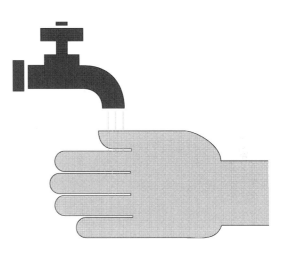

Primero, lavo mis manos.

Then I eat my food.

Después, como mi comida.

Afterwards, I clean the table.

Luego, limpio la mesa.

Table Activity:

What goes together?

Practice discussing category and function by drawing a line between the two items that go together.

Table Activity:

Who has more?

Circle the picture of the child who has more school items than his or her classmates.

Craft:
School Supplies Puzzle

Print two copies of the puzzle. Cut the pieces apart for one of the copies. For younger children, have the child match and glue or tape the pieces on top of the copy and color them.

Materials: scissors, glue or tape, crayons

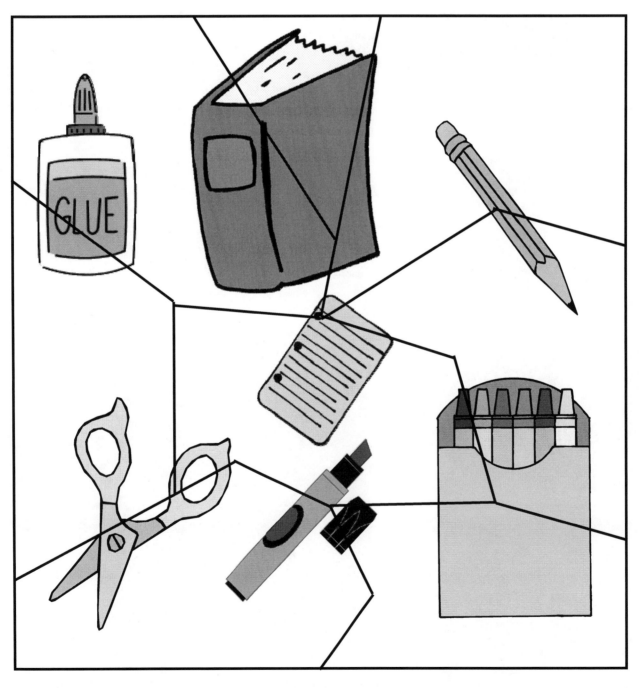

     Curriculum-Based Speech Therapy Activities

Craft:

What's in my Backpack?

Print out an extra copy of the surprise bag pictures. Cut a hole across the top of the backpack and tape a sandwich bag across the opening on the back. Take turns placing items in the back pack that are needed for school. Discuss what could/couldn't fit (i.e. a school bus is too big).

Materials: scissors, glue, tape, crayons, sandwich bag

Recipe:
School Bus Twinkie

Create a school bus out of a Twinkie. Prepare the activity by cutting one of the corners off of the top. Slice the corner in half horizontally and place the top part in the corner of the Twinkie to make the bus hood. Use frosting to stick the M&M wheels to the bus and create windows. See pictures on the following sequence page for guidance.

Materials: Twinkies, 4 M&Ms per Twinkie, frosting tube

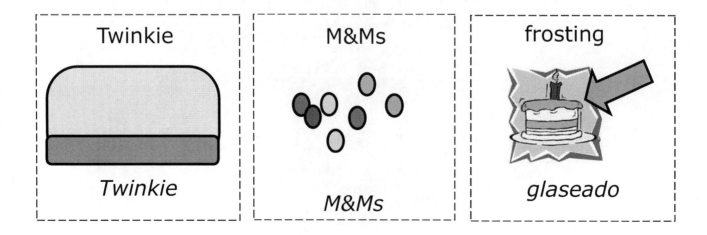

Curriculum-Based Speech Therapy Activities

Recipe:
School Bus Twinkie

J

SCHOOL

Use these sequencing cards to teach a child how to follow directions with this simple recipe.

Cut the corner of the Twinkie.

Corte la esquina del Twinkie.

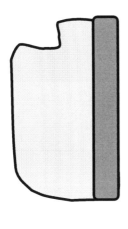

Use frosting for windows.

Utilice glaseado para las ventanas.

Get a Twinkie.

Agarre un Twinkie.

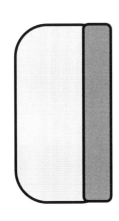

Put on 4 M&Ms for wheels.

Utilice 4 M&Ms para las ruedas.

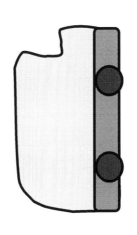

Game:

Following Directions Dice

Cut out the dice and tape them into a square. Have students throw both dice at the same time to create a silly instruction to follow.

Materials: scissors, tape, 2 chairs, table, door, book, pencil, tape, paper, block

FOLD TAB IN

on the floor

en el piso

on the chair

en la silla

FOLD TAB IN

entre las sillas

between the chairs

under the table

debajo de la mesa

In front of the teacher

En frente de la maestra

FOLD TAB IN

next to the door

al lado de la puerta

Game:
Following Directions Dice

K

SCHOOL

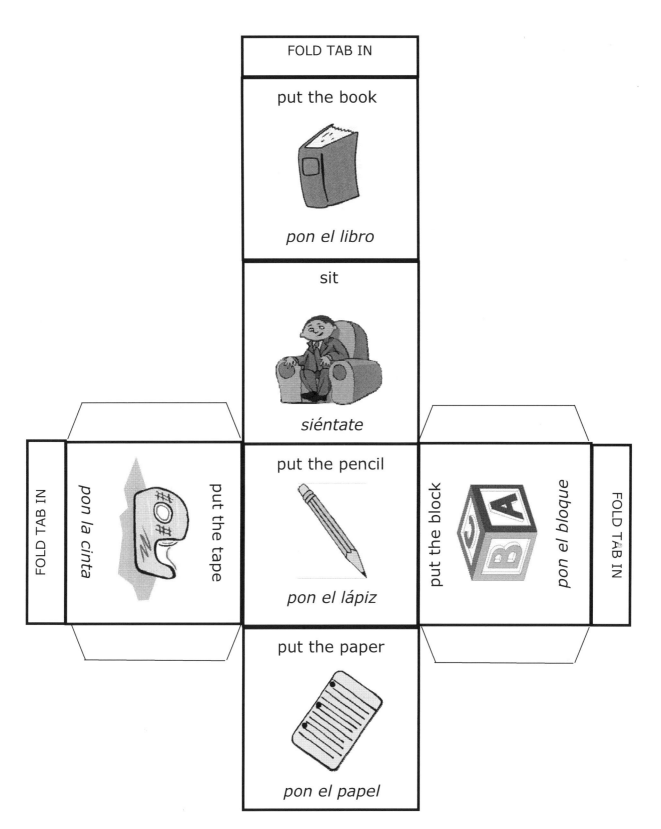

FOLD TAB IN

put the book

pon el libro

sit

siéntate

FOLD TAB IN

pon la cinta

put the tape

put the pencil

pon el lápiz

put the block

pon el bloque

FOLD TAB IN

put the paper

pon el papel

Parent Note:

School Coloring Page

L

SCHOOL

Hi Parents!

This week we are talking about things we use at school. Ask your child about what things are in his classroom and what they are used for.

¡Hola Padres!

Esta semana estamos hablando de cosas de la escuela. Pregúntele a su hijo acerca de las cosas que están en su salón y para que se utilizan.

Animals
Los animales

Animals / *Los animales*

SONGS

English	Spanish
The Farm	*La granja*
Octopus	*Un pulpito*
Five Little Monkeys	*Cinco monitos pequeños*
Color Farm	*Colores en la granja*
Old McDonald	*La granja del viejo McDonald*

Songs can be found at http://bilinguistics.com/music-for-speech-therapy/.

Book and Song Resources

BOOK LOCATOR

NON-FICTION

590
Zoological
Sciences/Animals

Title	Author
Brown Bear, Brown Bear, What Do You See? *¿Oso pardo, oso pardo, qué ves allí?*	E. Carle
From Head to Toe *De la cabeza a los pies*	E. Carle
I Went Walking *Salí de paseo*	S. Williams
Animals *Los animales*	C. Beaton
Animals *Animales*	E. Carl
Let's Go to the Farm *Vamos a la granja*	E.Weiss & L.C. Froeb

Animals Unit Content

Section	Schedule	Activity	Goals
A	Surprise Bag	Cut out animal picture cards Other options: • Plastic toy animals • Stuffed animals • Animal puppets	• Following directions • Utterance expansion • Answering questions • Turn taking
B	Articulation Station	Animal-related words organized by sound for articulation targets Record sounds for examples of correct productions	• Production of correct sounds in words and phrases
C	Phonology Syllable Strips	Animal picture cards in English and Spanish for 1– to 5-syllable words	• Syllable segmentation
D	Mini Book #1	Where Animals Live *Dónde viven los animales*	• Answering questions • Following directions • Sequencing • Utterance expansion
E	Mini Book #2	All About Animals! *¡Todo acerca de los animales!*	• Following directions • Sequencing • Utterance expansion • Part-whole relationships
F	Table Activity #1	Part and Whole Relationships	• Part-whole relationships • Labeling animals and parts • Utterance expansion

Animals Unit Content

Section	Schedule	Activity	Goals
G	Table Activity #2	Who's the Biggest One of All?	• Size concepts • Describing • Labeling
H	Craft #1	Africa Mobile	• Following directions • Labeling animals • Requesting materials
I	Craft #2	Paper Plate Masks	• Following directions • Basic concepts: part-whole, colors, number, shapes • Plurals (ear vs. ears)
J	Recipe	Animal Sponge Capsules	• Following directions • Requesting • Sequencing • Utterance expansion
K	Game	File Folder Game: Animal Homes	• Answering questions • Categorizing • Labeling • Utterance expansion
L	Parent Note	Animal Coloring Page	• Demonstrate learning • Give parents visual cues to understand and converse with their child

Curriculum-Based Speech Therapy Activities

Surprise Bag:
Animal Picture Cards

bat	bear	deer	crab
murciélago	*oso*	*venado*	*cangrejo*
whale	fish	octopus	shark
ballena	*pez*	*pulpo*	*tiburón*
snake	frog	fox	raccoon
víbora	*rana*	*zorro*	*mapache*
crow	turtle	squirrel	owl
cuervo	*tortuga*	*ardilla*	*búho*

Articulation Station

Use these words during any of the structured activities or in homework assignments to target a child's goals.

B

ANIMALS

English

M **m**onkey, **m**ouse, **m**a**mm**al, **m**oose, ani**m**al, fla**m**ingo, la**m**a

P **p**ig, **p**enguin, **p**latypus, **p**anda, chim**p**anzee, leo**p**ard, shee**p**

B **b**ear, **b**ird, **b**at, **b**ison, **b**a**b**oon, lo**b**ster, ra**bb**it, ze**b**ra, cra**b**

K **c**at, **c**ow, **k**angaroo, tur**k**ey, ra**cc**oon, tou**c**an, duc**k**, sna**k**e

G **g**oat, **g**azelle, **g**oose, kan**g**aroo, dra**g**on, ti**g**er, do**g**, fro**g**

T **t**urtle, **t**iger, **t**urkey, platypus, alliga**t**or, octopus, ca**t**, ba**t**, ra**t**

D **d**og, **d**uck, **d**eer, **d**olphin, pan**d**a, lizar**d**, bir**d**, leopar**d**, squi**d**

F **f**ish, **f**rog, **f**ox, **f**lamingo, bu**ff**alo, dol**ph**in, ele**ph**ant, gira**ff**e

S **s**nake, **s**eal, **s**loth, **s**kink, roo**s**ter, bi**s**on, hor**s**e, walru**s**, goo**s**e

L **l**izard, **l**ion, turt**l**e, **l**eopard, **l**emur, squirre**l**, ee**l**, came**l**, eag**l**e

R **r**abbit, **r**accoon, **r**at, **r**eptile, go**r**illa, squi**rr**el bea**r**, dee**r**, alligato**r**

Articulation Station

Use these words during any of the structured activities or in homework assignments to target a child's goals.

B

ANIMALS

Spanish

M   **m**ono, **m**urciélago, **m**apache, ani**m**al, cala**m**ar, cai**m**án, lla**m**a

P   **p**ulpo, **p**erro, **p**ato, **p**ez, **p**ollo, **p**ájaro, ma**p**ache, ser**p**iente

B   **b**allena, **b**úfalo, **b**úho, **b**urro, a**b**eja, ca**b**allo, ce**b**ra, ca**b**ra

K   **k**oala, **c**anguro, **c**aballo, **c**astor, **c**amello, **c**aracol, va**c**a, tu**c**án

G   **g**ato, **g**anso, **g**acela, **g**orila, ti**g**re, tortu**g**a, á**g**uila, murciéla**g**o

T   **t**igre, **t**ortuga, ga**t**o, cas**t**or, coyo**t**e, lagar**t**o, elefan**t**e, ra**t**ón

D   **d**elfín, **d**ingo, ar**d**illa, pan**d**a, arma**d**illo, coco**d**rilo, cer**d**o, vena**d**o

F   **f**oca, **f**lamenco, ele**f**ante, jira**f**a, mo**f**eta, del**f**ín, bú**f**alo

S   **c**ebra, **c**erdo, **c**iervo, ga**c**ela, mo**s**ca, al**c**e, o**s**o, pe**z**, avestru**z**

L   **l**obo, **l**oro, **l**agarto, **l**eón, a**l**ce, e**l**efante, águi**l**a, búfa**l**o, caraco**l**

R   **r**atón, **r**ata, **r**ana, bu**rr**o, a**r**dilla, to**r**tuga, lo**r**o, pája**r**o, hámste**r**

Phonology:

Syllable Strips in English

bear
◯

fish
◯

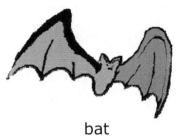

bat
◯

monkey
◯ ◯

turtle
◯ ◯

eagle
◯ ◯

kangaroo
◯ ◯ ◯

octopus
◯ ◯ ◯

elephant
◯ ◯ ◯

rhinoceros
◯ ◯ ◯ ◯

hippopotamus
◯ ◯ ◯ ◯ ◯

anaconda
◯ ◯ ◯ ◯

Curriculum-Based Speech Therapy Activities

Phonology:
Syllable Strips in Spanish

pez

◯

oso

◯ ◯

castor

◯ ◯

mono

◯ ◯

tortuga

◯ ◯ ◯

pájaro

◯ ◯ ◯

mapache

◯ ◯ ◯

tiburón

◯ ◯ ◯

víbora

◯ ◯ ◯

elefante

◯ ◯ ◯ ◯

murciélago

◯ ◯ ◯ ◯

rinocerante

◯ ◯ ◯ ◯ ◯

Mini Book:

Cut, color, and create a *WHERE* book about animals.

Where Animals Live

Donde viven los animales

Cows live on a farm.

Las vacas viven en una granja.

Raccoons live in the forest.

Los mapaches viven en el bosque.

Crabs live in the sea.

Los cangrejos viven en el mar.

Mini Book:

Cut, color, and create a book about animals.

All about Animals!

¡Todo acerca de los animales!

Draw my Spots!

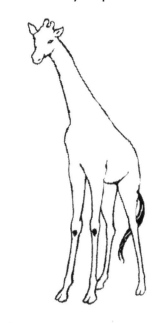

Dibuje mis manchas!

Connect the points to make my cage.

Une los puntos para hacer mi jaula con una linea.

Draw my wings. I want to fly!

Dibuje mis alas. ¡Quiero volar!

Table Activity:

Part-Whole Relationships

Match the animal to the body part and color if time permits.

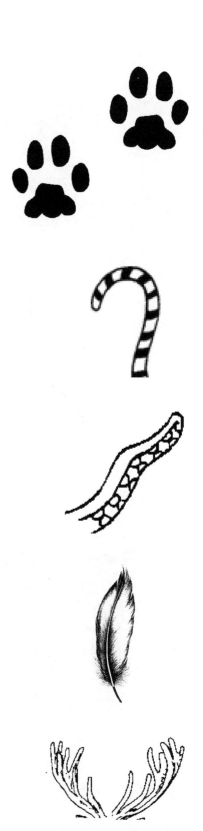

Curriculum-Based Speech Therapy Activities

Table Activity:

Who's the biggest one of all?

Circle the animal in each line that is the biggest.

Craft:

African Mobile

ANIMALS

Cut, color, and connect these animals into an African mobile. The easiest way is to tape the string to the back of each animal.

Materials: scissors, 7 pieces of string, tape, crayons

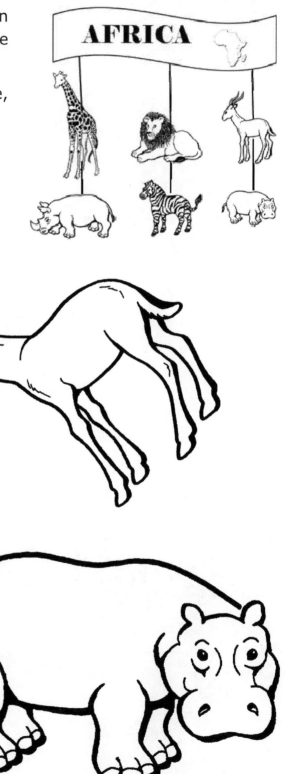

Craft:

African Mobile

Craft:

Animal Mask Making

We have given you several design ideas but be as creative as you want! Cut out the body parts from colored construction paper, and glue onto paper plates. Cut out circles for the eyes, and draw any additional lines.

Materials: paper plates, popsicle sticks or string, construction paper, markers

4 black circles, and 1 black triangle

2 brown circles, 2 smaller white circles, 1 brown triangle, 2 white rectangles, optional plate size brown circle

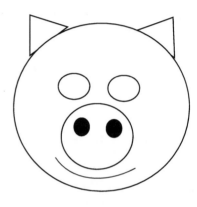

2 small black circles, one pink large circle, 2 pink triangles, optional plate-sized pink circle

8 orange triangles, 1 black triangle, optional plate-sized yellow circle

2 white half ovals, 1 pink heart

4 small black circles, 2 black half ovals, 2 yellow triangles, 1 yellow oval, 9 brown squares/spots, optional plate-sized yellow circle

Recipe:

Animal Sponge Capsules

Demonstrate a sponge growing in water or show an expanded sponge to increase your students' interest. Then, use the activity to take turns, identify colors, follow directions, and describe outcomes.

Materials: animal sponge capsules, water, a cup

Note* Warm or hot water makes sponges grow faster.

I want

Yo quiero

a cup

una taza

water

agua

a capsule

una pastilla

Game:
File folder game: Animal Homes

Cut out and paste pictures on the inside of a file folder. Use Velcro or putty to stick animal pictures from grab bag activity to their correct home (sky, land or water).

Note* Pictures will cover one and a half pages of the inside of the file folder. Use the extra room on the half page to mount the animals on Velcro or tape a baggie to keep the animals inside.

Materials: Two file folders, glue and Velcro or a baggie.

Game:

File Folder Game: Animal Homes

K

ANIMALS

Parent Note:

Animal Coloring Page

Hi Parents!

This week we are talking about animals. Ask your child to share what he knows about the animals in these scenes.

¡Hola Padres!

Esta semana estamos hablando de animales. Pregúntale a su hijo sobre cómo se llaman los animales y dónde viven.

Family
La familia

Family / La Familia

SONGS

English	Spanish
My Mother is a Baker	*Mi Mamá es panadera*
A Family is a Family	*¿Dónde está Papá?*
Cousins	*Primos*
Love, Love, Love My Family	*Es mi familia*
My Mommy	*Mí familia*

Songs can be found at http://bilinguistics.com/music-for-speech-therapy/.

Book and Song Resources

BOOK LOCATOR

NON-FICTION

306.8 Marriage and Family

Title	Author
We're Going on a Bear Hunt *Vamos a casar un oso*	M. Rosen
Does a Kangaroo Have a Mother Too? *¿El canguro tiene mamá?*	E. Carle
Froggy Bakes a Cake	J. London
My family and I *Mi familia y yo*	G. Rosa-Mendoza
Bear's Busy Family *La familia ocupada de Oso*	S. Blackstone

Family Unit Content

Section	Schedule	Activity	Goals
A	Surprise Bag	Cut out family member picture cards Other options: • People figures from playhouse • People puppets	• Following directions • Utterance expansion • Answering questions • Turn taking
B	Articulation Station	Family-related words organized by sound for articulation targets Record sounds for examples of correct productions	• Production of correct sounds in words and phrases
C	Phonology Syllable Strips	Family picture cards in English and Spanish for 1– to 5-syllable words	• Syllable segmentation
D	Mini Book #1	We Do Things Together! *¡Hacemos cosas juntos!*	• Answering questions • Verbs • Utterance expansion
E	Mini Book #2	My Family *Mi familia*	• Following directions • Naming • Utterance expansion • Numbers
F	Table Activity #1	Which ones are the same?	• Following directions • Same/different • Labeling • *Wh* and *yes/no* questions

Family Unit Content

Section	Schedule	Activity	Goals
G	Table Activity #2	Which Ones Are The Same?	• Prepositions • Spatial Relationships • Location
H	Craft #1	The People Who Live in My Home	• Following directions • Labeling family members • Requesting materials
I	Craft #2	Pets in My Family	• Following directions • Basic concepts: part-whole, colors, numbers • Plurals (ear vs. ears) • Requesting materials
J	Recipe	Pretzel House	• Following directions • Requesting • Sequencing • Utterance expansion
K	Game	File Folder Game: Family Categories	• Answering questions • Categorizing • Labeling • Utterance expansion
L	Parent Note	Family Coloring Page	• Demonstrate learning • Give parents visual cues to understand and converse with their child

Curriculum-Based Speech Therapy Activities

Surprise Bag:
Family Picture Cards

mom	dad	brothers	sisters
mamá	*papá*	*hermanos*	*hermanas*
grandma	grandpa	baby	family
abuela	*abuelo*	*bebé*	*familia*
cousins	nanny	uncle	aunt
primos	*niñera*	*tío*	*tía*
twins	cat	dog	house
gemelas	*gato*	*perro*	*casa*

Articulation Station

Use these words during any of the structured activities or in homework assignments to target a child's goals.

B
___
FAMILY

English

M   **m**o**m**, **m**other, **m**arry, grand**m**a, ho**m**e

P   **p**et, **p**arents, **p**lay, **p**arty, grand**p**a

B   **b**a**b**y, **b**rother, **b**ird, hus**b**and

K   **k**iss, **c**at, **c**are, **c**ousin

G   **g**randma, **g**randpa, en**g**aged, hu**g**, do**g**

T   sis**t**er, daugh**t**er, pe**t**, aun**t**

D   **d**aughter, **d**a**d**, **d**og, bir**d**, relate**d**, chil**d**, husban**d**

F   **f**ish, **f**amily, **f**iancé, ne**ph**ew, wi**f**e

S   **s**i**s**ter, **s**pou**s**e, **s**on, ki**ss**, nie**c**e

L   **l**ove, **l**ive, unc**l**e, re**l**ated, chi**l**d

R   **r**elative, g**r**andma, g**r**andpa, b**r**othe**r**, siste**r**, daughte**r**

Articulation Station

Use these words during any of the structured activities or in homework assignments to target a child's goals.

B
FAMILY

Spanish

M   **m**a**m**á, ge**m**elas, a**m**or, pri**m**o

P   **p**a**p**á, **p**erro, **p**rimo, **p**adrino, **p**rometido, **p**ez

B   **b**eso, **b**isa**b**uela, a**b**uelo, a**b**razo

K   **c**asa, **c**asar, **c**uidar

G   **g**ato, ten**g**o, ju**g**ar

T   **t**ío, **t**ía, **t**engo, **t**rizillos, masco**t**a

D   pa**d**rino, prometi**d**o, casa**d**o, cui**d**ar

F   **f**amilia, **f**eliz, **f**iesta

S   **s**obrino, **s**obrina, e**s**po**s**a, ca**s**ado, ca**s**a, be**s**o, pe**z**

L   abue**l**o, abue**l**a, geme**l**as

R   he**r**mano, he**r**mana, ab**r**azo, p**r**imo, p**r**ima, amo**r**, cuida**r**

Phonology:

Syllable Strips in English

mom

dad

son

sister

brother

daughter

family

reunion

grandfather

stepsister

great grandfather

great grandmother

Curriculum-Based Speech Therapy Activities

Phonology:
Syllable Strips in *Spanish*

pez

◯

tío

◯ ◯

tía

◯ ◯

mamá

◯ ◯

papá

◯ ◯

casa

◯ ◯

abuelo

◯ ◯ ◯

gemelas

◯ ◯ ◯

trillizos

◯ ◯ ◯

bisabuelo

◯ ◯ ◯

prometido

◯ ◯ ◯ ◯

embarazada

◯ ◯ ◯ ◯ ◯

Mini Book:

Cut, color, and create a book about what you do with your family.

D

FAMILY

We Do Things Together!

¡Hacemos cosas juntos!

We eat dinner.

Comemos la cena.

We go shopping.

Vamos de compras.

We play outside.

Jugamos fuera.

Mini Book:

Glue photos or draw pictures of people in your family. Make extra copies of the bottom two pages as needed.

E

FAMILY

My Family

Mi familia

I have ____ people in my family.

Hay ____ personas en mi familia.

_____ is my _____.

_____ *es mi* _____.

_____ is my _____.

_____ *es mi* _____.

www.bilinguistics.com

95

Table Activity:

Which ones are the same?

Circle the family members in each line that are the same.

Table Activity:
Prepositions

Draw a line from a box to a family member that matches the preposition, and talk about where the family members are.

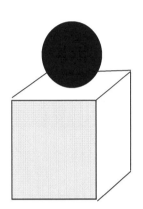

On top

Encima

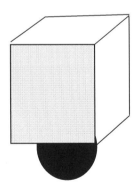

Under

Debajo

Craft:
The People Who Live in My Home

H

FAMILY

Cut, color, and glue the family members from the surprise bag pictures into the house. You may use photographs instead.

Materials: scissors, glue/tape, crayons

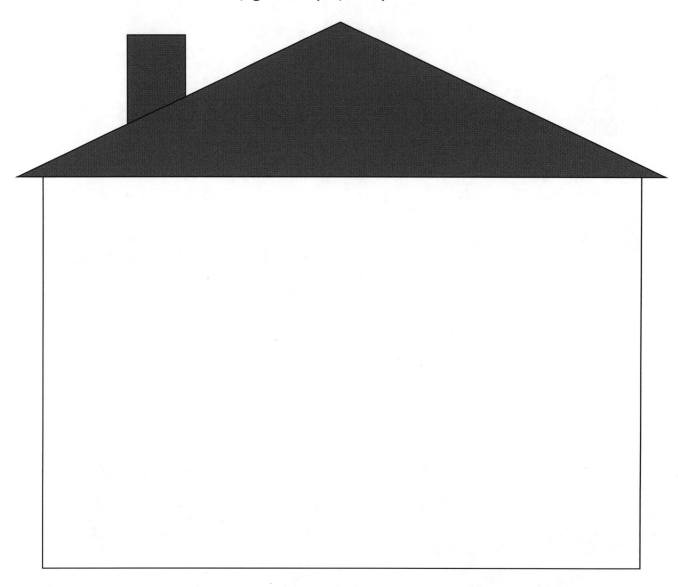

Note to parent: Today we talked about who lives in our house. After cutting and gluing family members in the house, ask your child who lives in their house. Have them say one word (ex: "mommy") or a complete phrase (ex: "Mommy lives in my house."

Hoy hablamos de las personas que viven en nuestras casas. Después de cortar y pegar las personas en la casa, haga preguntas a su hijo(a) sobre quien vive en su casa. Puede usar una palabra sola (ej: "mamá") o una frase completa (ej: "Mamá vive en mi casa").

Craft:
Pets in My Family

Make a pet puppet by gluing parts onto popsicle sticks.

Materials: scissors, crayons glue, popsicle sticks

Die-cut/pre-cut shapes: large circle for heads plus circles, ovals, triangles for body parts

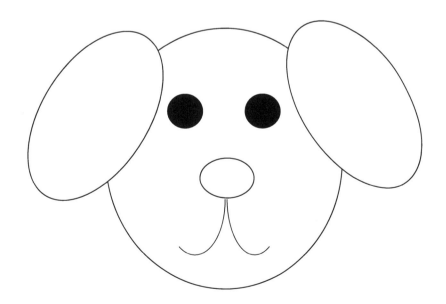

Recipe:

Pretzel House

Use bread, peanut butter and pretzel sticks to make a house snack. Take two slices of bread. Cut one piece diagonally to make two triangles. Discard one triangle or use it as your example. Spread peanut butter on the bread and add pretzels as outlines or horizontal logs. Your students can also add a chimney. Have children request different foods to build their house.

Materials: bread, peanut butter, pretzel sticks

I want

Yo quiero

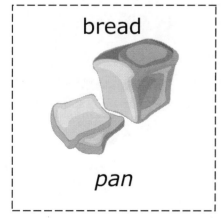

bread

pan

peanut butter

crema de cacahuate

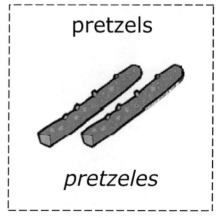

pretzels

pretzeles

Recipe:

Pretzel House

FAMILY

Use this recipe to practice following directions and make a delicious snack as a reward.

Spread peanut butter on the bread.

Unta crema de cacahuate sobre el pan.

Make a triangle roof using two pretzels.

Haz un techo triangular usando dos pretzels.

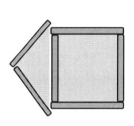

Get a slice of bread.

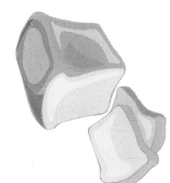

Agarre una rebanda de pan.

Make a square house using four pretzels.

Haz una casa cuadrada usando cuatro pretzels.

Game:

File Folder Game: Family/Categories

Cut out and paste pictures (2 per side) on the inside of a file folder. Use Velcro or putty to stick foods, colors, animals, and sports in proper categories and ask them if they know what each family member likes.

Materials: one folder, glue, Velcro.

| red | blue | pink | purple | ? |

Game:

File Folder Game: Family/Categories

FAMILY

Colors
Colores

Sports
Deportes

Game:

File Folder Game: Family/Categories

Food

Comida

Pets

Mascotas

Parent Note:

Family Coloring Page

Hi Parents!

This week we are talking about family. Discuss what each family member likes to do or what they do during the day. You can also discuss how family members are related or where they live.

¡Hola Padres!

Esta semana estamos hablando de la familia. Platiquen con su hijo sobre cada miembro de la familia y lo que le gusta hacer o lo que hace durante el día. También, puede hablar sobre cómo están relacionados los miembros de la familia y dónde viven.

Fall

El otoño

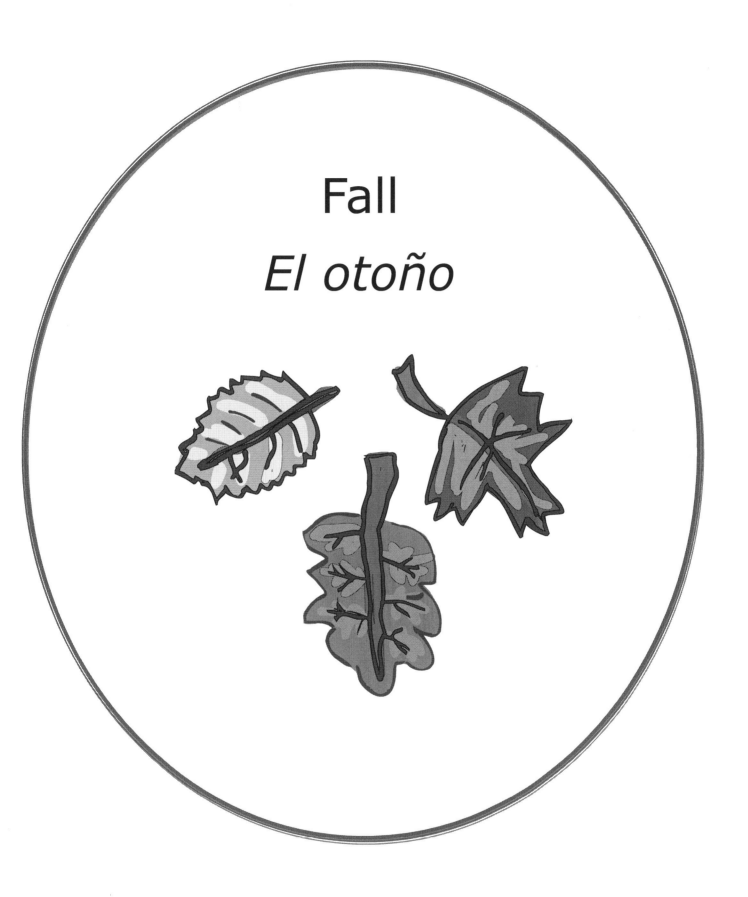

Fall / El otoño

SONGS

English	Spanish
Weather Song	*La cancion del tiempo*
Autumn Leaves are Falling Down	En otoño caen las hojas
Leaves on the Tree	*Hojas, hojas*
Way High up in an Apple Tree	*¿Cuántas manzanas hay?*
Five Little Pumpkins	*Cinco calabazas*

Songs can be found at http://bilinguistics.com/music-for-speech-therapy/.

Book and Song Resources

BOOK LOCATOR

NON-FICTION

508.2
Autumn

Title	Author
We're Going on a Leaf Hunt	S. Metzger
Leaf Man	L. Ehlert
I See Fall	
Veo el otoño	C. Ghigna
Leaves in Fall	
Las hojas en otoño	E.H. Rustad
El circulo de las calabazas	G. Levenson
The Little Old Lady Who Was Not Afraid of Anything	
La viejecita que no le tenía miedo de nada	L. Williams

Fall Unit Content

Section	Schedule	Activity	Goals
A	Surprise Bag	Cut out fall picture cards Other options: colored leaves from outside	• Following directions • Utterance expansion • Answering questions • Turn taking
B	Articulation Station	Fall-related words organized by sound for articulation targets Record sounds for examples of correct productions	• Production of correct sounds in words and phrases
C	Phonology Syllable Strips	Fall picture cards in English and Spanish for 1– 6 syllable words	• Syllable segmentation
D	Mini Book #1	What we do in fall *Lo que hacemos en el otoño*	• Answering questions • Following directions • Utterance expansion
E	Mini Book #2	Leaves fall down! *¡Las hojas se caen!*	• Following directions • Utterance expansion • Descriptions
F	Table Activity #1	Pumpkin Life Cycle *El ciclo de vida de la calabaza*	• Sequencing • Labeling • Utterance expansion

Fall Unit Content

Section	Schedule	Activity	Goals
G	Table Activity #2	Leaf Sort	• Describing • Following directions • Utterance expansion • Size concepts
H	Craft #1	Paper Bag Scarecrow	• Following directions • Requesting materials • Basic concepts • Plurals (arm vs. arms)
I	Craft #2	Fall Tree	• Following directions • Basic concepts: colors, number • Describing
J	Recipe	Pumpkin Play Doh	• Following directions • Requesting • Sequencing • Utterance expansion
K	Game	File Folder Game: Fall Fun	• Answering questions • Categorizing • Labeling • Utterance expansion
L	Parent Note	Fall Coloring Page	• Demonstrate learning • Give parents visual cues to understand and converse with their child

Surprise Bag:
Fall Picture Cards

leaf	tree	rake	apple
hoja	*árbol*	*rastrillo*	*manzana*
acorn	pile	squirrel	jacket
bellota	*montón*	*ardilla*	*chaqueta*
wind	dessert	cold	pants
viento	*postre*	*frío*	*pantalones*
pumpkin	pumpkin patch	scarecrow	harvest
calabaza	*huerta*	*espantapájaros*	*cosecha*

Articulation Station

Use these words during any of the structured activities or in homework assignments to target a child's goals.

B

FALL

English

M   **m**ake, pu**m**pkin, **m**unch, **m**ischief, **m**edium, **m**easure, **m**om

P   **p**ile, a**pp**le, **p**umpkin **p**ie, **p**atch, **p**ants, **p**lay, **p**eople, **p**retend

B   **b**ury, **b**uild, **b**oy, **b**low, **b**ig, **b**utton, **b**ake, **b**uy, **b**oat,

K   a**c**orn, **s**carecrow, pump**k**in, jac**k**et, **c**olors, s**q**uirrel, ra**k**e, **c**old

G   **g**ate, **g**olden, bi**g**, **g**oose, **g**uess, **g**irl, **g**ather, **g**oop, **g**ive

T   **t**ree, jacke**t**, **t**ake, **t**ool, **t**reat, **t**runk, **t**ear, **t**op

D   col**d**, **d**og, **d**amp, **d**ump, **d**ecorate, **d**ig, **d**estroy, **d**amage

F   **f**all, **f**lower, **f**estival, **f**un, **f**air, **f**ree, **f**ace, **f**lu, **f**ly, **f**riends, **f**ruit

S   **s**carecrow, leave**s**, **s**quirrel, **s**prout, **s**eed, **s**urprise

L   **l**eaf, squirre**l**, **l**eap, **l**ay, **l**eaves, **l**earn, **l**augh, **l**ake

R   aco**r**n, **r**ake, t**r**ee, **r**un, **r**ich, **r**oll, **r**ace, **r**ip

Articulation Station

Use these words during any of the structured activities or in homework assignments to target a child's goals.

B

FALL

Spanish

M   **m**anzana, **m**ontón , **m**ediana, **m**ucho, **m**edir, **m**amá

P   es**p**anta**p**ájaros, **p**astel de calabaza, **p**antalones, **p**reparar

B   ár**b**ol, cala**b**aza, **v**iento, **b**rote, **b**uscar, **b**rincar, **b**ellota, **v**er

K   **c**alabaza, **c**aer, cha**q**ueta, chi**q**uito, **c**orrer, es**c**onder, **c**reer

G   **g**rande, **g**ordo, ju**g**ar, **g**ato, **g**usano, **g**ritar, a**g**arrar, **g**ripe, ami**g**o

T   vien**t**o, chaque**t**a, ras**t**rillo, bello**t**a, mon**t**ón , chaque**t**a, espan**t**apájaros, huer**t**o, chiqui**t**o

D   ar**d**illa, **d**ora**d**o, **d**ía, ayu**d**ar, **d**ecorar, **d**estruir, **d**año, **d**elicioso

F   **f**lor, **f**río, **f**estival, **f**eria, **f**avorito, **f**inca, **f**ingir, **f**ruta,

S   **s**onrisa, **s**ol, **s**emilla, hoja**s**, man**z**ana, calaba**z**a, **s**orpresa

L   **l**uz, árbo**l**, calabaza, pantalones, **l**ámpara, **l**impiar

R   a**r**dilla, **r**astrillo, hue**r**to, co**rr**er, es**c**onde**r**, **r**ecoger, **r**ico, **r**odar

Phonology:
Syllable Strips in English

leaf

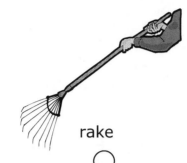

rake

tree

pile

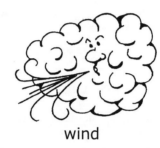

wind

scarecrow

pumpkin

jacket

squirrel

acorn

harvest

apple

Curriculum-Based Speech Therapy Activities

Phonology:
Syllable Strips in Spanish

montón
○ ○

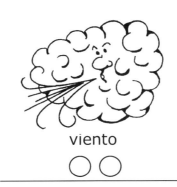

viento
○ ○

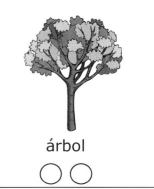

árbol
○ ○

hoja
○ ○

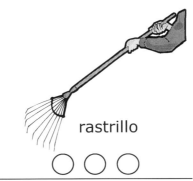

rastrillo
○ ○ ○

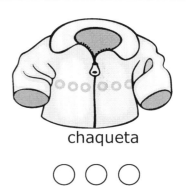

chaqueta
○ ○ ○

bellota
○ ○ ○

ardilla
○ ○ ○

cosecha
○ ○ ○

manzana
○ ○ ○

calabaza
○ ○ ○ ○

espantapájaros
○ ○ ○ ○ ○ ○

Mini Book:

Cut, color, and create a *WHAT* book about fall.

WHAT we do in fall

QUÉ hacemos

en el otoño

I put on my jacket.

Me pongo la chaqueta.

I pick out pumpkins.

Escogo calabazas.

I play in the leaves with my friends.

Juego en las hojas con mis amigos.

Curriculum-Based Speech Therapy Activities

Mini Book:

Cut, color, and create a book about leaves.

Leaves fall down!

¡Las hojas se caen!

This is a red leaf.

Ésta es una hoja roja.

This is an orange leaf.

Ésta es una hoja anaranjada.

The leaves fall down!

¡Las hojas se caen!

Table Activity:

Pumpkin Life Cycle

Students sequence the parts of a pumpkin's life cycle in order from "first" to "last." Encourage students to label and describe as they engage with the materials.

Materials: image of pumpkin seed (la semilla), plant (la planta), flower (la flor), pumpkin (la calabaza)

First	Next

Primero	*Luego*
Then	**Last**

Después	*Al final*

Table Activity:

Leaf sort

Students can work as a team or 1:1 with you to sort leaves according to size.

Materials: cut outs or real leaves of different sizes

big/*grande*

medium/*mediana*

small/pequeña

Craft:

Paper Bag Scarecrow

This scarecrow is super fun to make! It can be easily paired with <u>The Little Old Lady Who Was Not Afraid of Anything</u> by adding more clothing items made from construction paper.

Materials: brown paper bag, popsicle sticks, black marker, glue, red, orange, yellow and green construction paper

Curriculum-Based Speech Therapy Activities

Craft:
Fall Tree

Students love to get their hands dirty. With some newspaper to cover the table and a smock or an old t-shirt to keep clothing clean, finger painting fall colored leaves is an easy way for students to create beautiful artwork.

Materials: construction paper, marker, paints, newspaper, smocks or old t-shirts

Craft:

Fall Tree

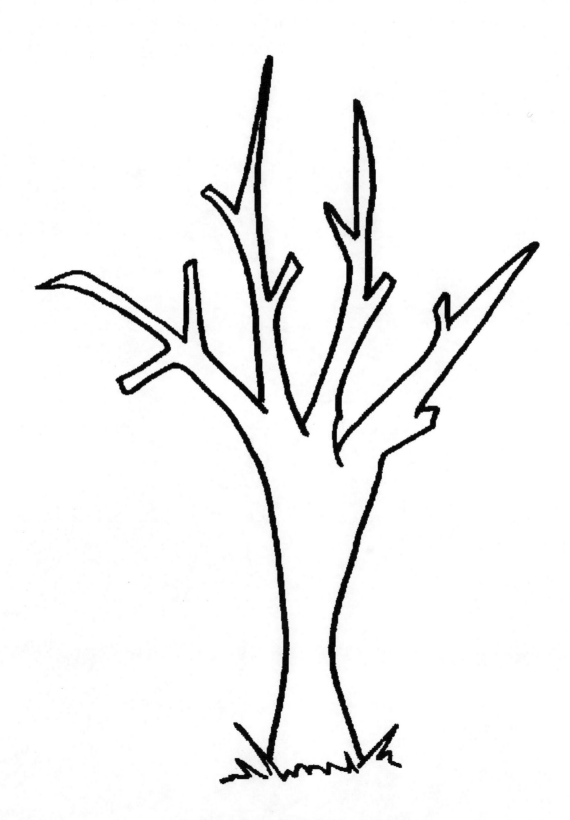

Recipe:

Pumpkin Play Doh

This easy to make pumpkin Play Doh is a fun way to engage children in multisensory learning!

Materials: 2 cups plain flour, 1 cup salt, 1 tbsp. oil, 1 cup cold water, liquid food coloring, pumpkin pie spice, or a blend of cinnamon, nutmeg, ginger, and cardamom

Add water and food coloring to the bowl.

Añada agua y colorante al plato hondo.

Add the spices and smell!

¡Añada las especias y huele!

Combine flour and salt in a bowl.

Combine la harina y la sal en un plato hondo.

Knead the dough.

Amase la masa.

Recipe:

Pumpkin Play Doh

J

FALL

I want

Yo quiero

---

a bowl

un plato hondo

---

water

agua

---

flour and salt

harina y sal

---

drops of coloring

gotas de colorante

---

spices

especias

---

to smell

oler

124

Curriculum-Based Speech Therapy Activities

Game:

File Folder Game: Fall Fun

Cut out and paste pictures on the inside of a file folder. Use Velcro or putty to stick activities to their respective season.

Materials: two file folders, Velcro or putty, a plastic sandwich bag

Game:

File Folder Game: Fall Fun

K

FALL

Fall activities/*Actividades del otoño*

Summer activities/*Actividades del verano*

Curriculum-Based Speech Therapy Activities

Parent Note:

Fall Coloring Page

L

FALL

Hi Parents!

In speech therapy, we are talking about fall! Ask your child to share what he knows about the activities we do in fall to practice his/her communication.

¡Hola Padres!

En la terapia del habla, estamos hablando del otoño. Platiquen con su hijo sobre las actividades que hacemos en el otoño para practicar su comunicación.

Friends
Los amigos

Friends / Los amigos

SONGS

English	Spanish
Hello Friend	*Hola amigo*
Special Me	*Yo soy especial*
If You're Happy	*Si usted está feliz*
Goodbye Friends	*Adios amigos*

Songs can be found at http://bilinguistics.com/music-for-speech-therapy/.

Book and Song Resources

BOOK LOCATOR

NON-FICTION

177.62
Friendship

Title	Author
A Color of His Own *Su propio color*	L. Lionni
Elmer's Friends *Los amigos de Elmer*	D. McKee
Margaret and Margarita *Margarita y Margaret*	L. Reiser
Big Dog...Little Dog *Perro grande...perro pequeño*	P.D. Eastman
Should I Share My Ice Cream?	M. Willems
We're Different, We're the Same	B. Kates
That's What a Friend Is	P.K. Hallinan

Friends Unit Content

Section	Schedule	Activity	Goals
A	Surprise Bag	Cut out friend picture cards Other options: • Use pictures of your students playing together • Use student photos	• Following directions • Utterance expansion • Answering questions • Turn taking
B	Articulation Station	Friend-related words organized by sound for articulation targets Record sounds for examples of correct productions	• Production of correct sounds in words and phrases
C	Phonology Syllable Strips	Friend picture cards in English and Spanish for 1– to 5-syllable words	• Syllable segmentation
D	Mini Book #1	Where Friends Play *Donde juegan los amigos*	• Answering questions • Following directions • Utterance expansion
E	Mini Book #2	I Share with My Friends! *¡Comparto con mis amigos!*	• Answering questions • Following directions • Utterance expansion
F	Table Activity #1	Categorization	• Semantic group relationships • Labeling objects and category names • Utterance expansion

Friends Unit Content

Section	Schedule	Activity	Goals
G	Table Activity #2	How do you feel when...?	• Perspective-taking • Describing • Labeling
H	Craft #1	Friendship Flag	• Following directions • Turn-taking • Requesting materials
I	Craft #2	Crown of Friends	• Following directions • Basic concepts: colors, number, shapes • Adjectives
J	Recipe	Friendship Fruit Salad	• Following directions • Requesting • Sequencing • Utterance expansion
K	Game	File Folder Game: Find a Friend	• Turn-taking • Following directions • Describing • Utterance expansion
L	Parent Note	Friends Coloring Page	• Demonstrate learning • Give parents visual cues to understand and converse with their child

Curriculum-Based Speech Therapy Activities

Surprise Bag:
Friend Picture Cards

Our friends are:/*Nuestros amigos están:*

sharing	laughing	reading	shooting
compartiendo	*riéndose*	*leyendo*	*encestando*
taking a picture	taking turns	talking	swinging
tomando una foto	*tomando turnos*	*hablando*	*balanceando*
dressing up	jumping	building	smiling
disfrazándose	*brincando*	*construyendo*	*sonriendo*
throwing	acting	running	playing
tirando	*actuando*	*corriendo*	*jugando*

Articulation Station

Use these words during any of the structured activities or in homework assignments to target a child's goals.

B

FRIENDS

English

M   **m**ake, **m**y, ti**m**e, sa**m**e, fa**m**ily

P   **p**lay, hel**p**, su**pp**ort

B   **b**oy, **b**ooks, **b**asket**b**all, super**b**

K   **c**limb, **c**ommuni**c**ation, ma**k**e, **c**are, **c**hameleon

G   **g**reet, **g**irl, **g**ame, **g**enerous, play**g**round, fla**g**

T   par**t**y, **t**ogether, apprecia**t**e

D   **d**raw, sa**d**, frien**d**ship, han**d**prints

F   **f**riend, **f**lag, **f**un, di**ff**erent, lau**gh**

S   **s**lide, **s**wings, under**s**tand

L   **l**augh, **l**earn, chame**l**eon, ba**ll**

R   sha**r**e, party, **r**ecess

Articulation Station

Use these words during any of the structured activities or in homework assignments to target a child's goals.

B

FRIENDS

Spanish

M   a**m**igo, **m**is, a**m**able, fa**m**ilia

P   **p**arque, colum**p**io, a**p**render

B   **v**ecino, **b**andera, ama**b**le

K   **c**ompartir, **c**olumpio, a**c**tividad

G   ami**g**o, ju**g**ar, jue**g**o, **g**anar

T   diver**t**ido, compar**t**ir, fies**t**a, jun**t**os, **t**odos

D   amista**d**, ban**d**era, **d**ivertido

F   **f**eliz, **f**enomenal, **f**iel, di**f**erente

S   **s**aludar, **s**onreír, ha**c**er, feli**z,** re**s**baladía, ami**s**tad, junto**s**

L   columpios, resba**l**adía, **l**ibros, pie**l**, fie**l**

R   **r**esbaladía, juga**r**, reí**r,** sonreí**r**, gene**r**oso, aprecia**r**

Phonology:
Syllable Strips in English

flag
◯
_____

slide
◯
_____

friends
◯
_____

playground
◯ ◯
_____

neighbor
◯ ◯
_____

party
◯ ◯
_____

materials
◯ ◯ ◯ ◯
_____

basketball
◯ ◯ ◯
_____

together
◯ ◯ ◯
_____

activities
◯ ◯ ◯ ◯
_____

communicate
◯ ◯ ◯ ◯
_____

chameleon
◯ ◯ ◯ ◯
_____

Phonology:
Syllable Strips in Spanish

mío

◯

parque

◯ ◯

juntos

◯ ◯

felíz

◯ ◯

compartir

◯ ◯ ◯

amigos

◯ ◯ ◯

bandera

◯ ◯ ◯

saludar

◯ ◯ ◯

vecino

◯ ◯ ◯

columpio

◯ ◯ ◯

resbaladero

◯ ◯ ◯ ◯ ◯

actividades

◯ ◯ ◯ ◯ ◯

Mini Book:

Cut, color, and create a *WHERE* book about where we go with our friends.

Where Friends Play

Donde juegan los amigos

Friends play on the slide.

Los amigos juegan en la resbaladero.

Friends play on the swings.

Los amigos juegan en los columpios.

Friends play together!

¡Los amigos juegan juntos!

Mini Book:

Cut, color, and create a WHAT book about friends.

I Share with My Friends!

¡Comparto con mis amigos!

I share materials.

Comparto los materiales.

I share my books.

Comparto mis libros.

I like sharing with my friends!

¡Me gusta compartir con mis amigos!

Table Activity:
Categorization

Match the item to the category and color, if time permits.

Table Activity:

How do you feel when...?

Match the emotions to the scenarios.

FRIENDS

When my friend.../*Cuando mi amigo...*

shares toys/*comparte juguetes*

yells at me/*me grita*

kicks me/*me patea*

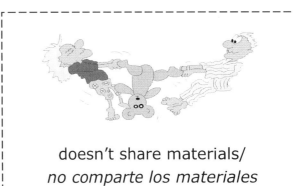

doesn't share materials/
no comparte los materiales

I feel.../*Me siento...*

happy / *feliz*

sad / *triste*

angry / *enojado*

afraid / *asustado*

Craft:

Friendship Flag

Show an example of a flag. Explain that it is a symbol for a country. It reminds us to get along and work together. Tell the students that they will make a friendship flag.

How to: The children work together and take turns placing their handprints on the strips of paper.

Once all the strips are finished, glue them to the larger piece of paper.

The children again take turns pasting the star with their name on it in the upper left corner of the flag.

During the activity, discuss how friends work together, take turns, and have fun together. Ask the children how they feel when their friends share and take turns.

Materials: finger paint, a large sheet of paper, wide strips of different colored paper, stars with children's names, glue

Curriculum-Based Speech Therapy Activities

Craft: Friendship Flag

Craft:
Crown of Friends

FRIENDS

Show an example of a finished crown. Explain that the friends are holding hands because they care about one another.

How to: Cut out the crown template. Glue or tape the people to a headband. Create up to five people holding hands. You can add hair or hats and vary the activity by making a crown of family members or a crown of different occupations. For younger students, sometimes it is easier to make crowns that only have two people rather than five stapled to a band of construction paper so they can create it faster and you can fit it to their head easier.

Use construction paper, crayons and glitter glue to add hair, faces, and clothes to each person. Decorate the base of the crown with glue and glitter to make designs. Staple or tape the ends of the crown together to wear!

Materials: construction paper, construction paper, crayons, glitter glue or puffy paint, scissors, stapler

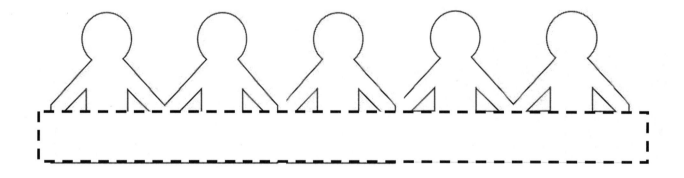

Craft:

Crown of Friends

I ♥ FRIENDS

Recipe:

Friendship Fruit Salad

Begin by telling students that the big bowl is like our classroom and that there are many important things that our room needs, especially good friends.

As you have the students take turns adding the fruit, explain what each fruit represents. You can be creative by using different fruits to talk about the different traits you want to   promote in your students.

For example:

-strawberry slices: good helpers and friends inside and outside the classroom

-mandarin oranges: hard workers who always try their best in everything they do

-pineapple chunks: share and take turns; care about each other

-grapes: kind, sweet words being said in our classroom, such as "please" and "thank you." They are also words of encouragement like "You can do it!"

Materials: large bowl, mixing spoon, plastic cups or small bowls, plastic spoons, sliced strawberries, grapes, mandarin oranges, pineapple, requesting visual (see opposite page)

a grape
una uva

a strawberry
una *fresa*

I want

Yo quiero

a cup
un vaso

Game:

File Folder Game: Find a Friend

K
FRIENDS

Have the student take turns with you or another classmate to find different pictures on one another's boards. For example, say, "Find a friend who is reading," or "Find the friends who are holding hands." Then, the student locates the image and hands it to you or his/her classmate.

Materials: one file folder, Velcro or one plastic sandwich bag

Game:

File Folder Game: Find a Friend

K

FRIENDS

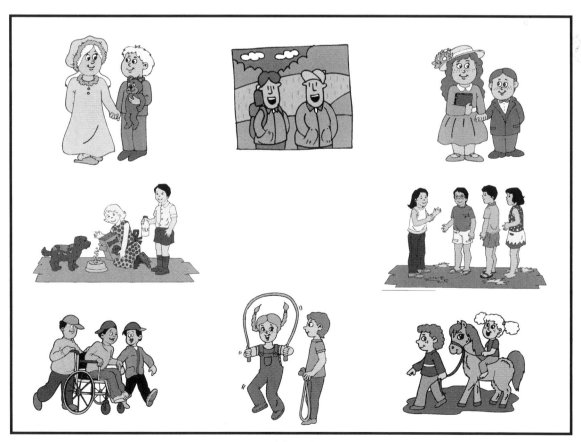

Parent Note:
Friends Coloring Page

L
FRIENDS

Hi Parents!

This week we are talking about friends. Use these images to talk with your child about what we do when we are playing with friends. Ask him to describe activities, name friends, and tell you where he plays with them.

¡Hola Padres!

Esta semana estamos hablando de los amigos. Utilicen estos dibojos para platicar con su hijo sobre cómo jugar bien con sus amigos. Pregúntale que actividades él hace, con quién juega, y dónde juega con ellos.

REFERENCES

Beckwith, L. & Cohen, S.E. (1989). Maternal responsiveness with preterm infants and later competency. In M.H. Bornstein (Ed.). *Maternal responsiveness: Characteristics and consequences: New directions for child development* (pp. 75-87). San Francisco: Jossey Bass.

Dempsey, I., & Dunst, C.J. (2004). Help-giving styles as a function of parent empowerment in families with a young child with a disability. *Journal of Intellectual and Developmental Disability*, *29*, 50-61.

Frey, K. S., Fewell, R. R., & Vadasy, P. F. (1989). The relationship between changes in parental adjustment and child outcome in families of young handicapped children. *Topics in Early Childhood Special Education, 8*, (4), 38 -57.

Krauss, M.W. (1993). Child-related and parenting stress: Similarities and differences between mothers and fathers of children with disabilities. *American Journal on Mental Retardation*, *97,* (4), 393-404.

Rogoff, B. (1990). *Apprenticeship in Thinking*. Oxford: Oxford University Press.

Rosetti, L. (2006). *The Rosetti Infant-Toddler Language Scale*. East Moline, IL: LinguiSystems, Inc.

Tomasello, M., & Farrar, MJ. (1986). Joint attention and early language. *Child Development*, *57,* (6), 1454-1463.

Vygotsky, L.S. (1967). Play and its role in the mental development of the child. *Soviet Psychology, 5*, 6-18.

Made in the USA
Columbia, SC
26 January 2025

52698320R00083